Calamities!

Calamities!

Jane Arthur

TE HERENGA WAKA
UNIVERSITY PRESS

Te Herenga Waka University Press
Victoria University of Wellington
PO Box 600 Wellington
teherengawakapress.co.nz

A catalogue record is available at the National Library
of New Zealand.

ISBN 9781776920723

Published with the support of a grant from

Printed in Singapore by Markono Print Media Pte Ltd

for Grisham

Contents

Risk Assessment

The Better to See You With, My Dear

This apocalypse is more boring
than Hollywood had prepared me for.

Yes, I'm scared, but constant worry
gets tiresome in its own way.

Part of the end
of the world is watching people claim

there comes a time when we should
let happen

the things that are going to happen.
I want to mess with the space–

time continuum, I want to shout,
But what if it doesn't have to! and

fuck with the future just because.
Just because I don't want to go out

in this horrifying slow-burning blaze.
Let me die normally or not at all.

Meteorite

A piece of what looked to me like rock
or concrete but which was in fact a slab
of a meteorite so old it pre-dates our
solar system gave me no chills or sense
of awe, which made me feel dead.
I think there's something wrong with me,
I thought, scrolling down, down, and
stopping on a clip of a dog walking
on its hind legs, eyes wide, nothing-to-see-here.
It looped a dozen times, never not funny,
and I laughed until I cried. *Has my*
heart lost its way, I wondered, wiping my tears,
caring about only stupid things? I tried
to place myself in the context of the size
and history of the universe. Nothing. In
a former life perhaps I was a maid, a go-go
dancer, a great war nurse, a wife, perhaps
I drew in the dirt, invented fire. I tried
to place myself in the context of the current
world and came up with nothing.
In the context of my life, I suspected that
joy came only before or after apathy
and elation usually preceded a migraine.
Some years earlier, I'd babysat
a ten-year-old who said have you
ever thought about whether the universe
has no end because if it does have an end,
what does the edge of the universe look like?
And my chest tightened because no,
I hadn't thought about that and I didn't know

but trying to imagine where the universe ends
made me feel like my particles were bursting
into something new, until I exhaled with a
snort and did a gesture like *mind blown*

Dodge

It's like each day is each of us
carving through space using
our bodies, in between objects
and molecules. Even colliding,
we don't really touch. We live only
what is scientifically possible.
(Each moment is a calving
of me from you and you from me.)

//

Let's divide into groups based on
the answers to these questions:

Can you light a fire? Can you
place yourself correctly along this
continuum: Your Past–Your History?
Is there truly another without whom
you couldn't live or would it merely
hurt a little/lot? How long could you
survive given various circumstances?
Do you feel worry as a jolt to your heart?
Or a rage? Will you atone or will you
tend to the defensive?
What would you do if there
wasn't a choice to be made?

//

Do we live only to the limits
of our comprehension?
We will never know
what we don't. Alack.
Some of us
carry shame and others of us
probably should.

There Are Dead Flies

There are dead flies in many of the cups and glasses on the kitchen shelves. I found one when I heard bzzing, quietly echoed. It was on its last legs, spinning in the bottom of a shot glass. Witnessed its last words. I threw the carcass outside and replaced the glass on the shelf, registering that I would judge another for not washing the glass first and yet I didn't wash it. I will wash it. All it will take is removing the glass from the shelf and placing it next to the sink. I will wash it, and the others. Maybe one day I will live in a house with cupboards instead of shelves and the flies will die elsewhere.

No Offense

The cats' ears are torn and the men's baseball
caps are offensive, in a way that seems
brash and indignant but cowardly too.
The cats' fights throughout the night sound awfully
like the screams of children in agony.
They wander inside like nothing's happened.
They wear their bloodied ears like statement hats.
Smug, but avoiding eye contact, in case.

It is challenging to unravel a
tapestry when you can't even stitch one.
It is also hard to wait for someone
when you couldn't rightly point them out in
a line-up. Instead you could bat at moths
until they're dead, light the window at night.

Way, Truth and Life

I don't know about you, Prometheus,
but I think I'm ready to set down my tools
and take a nap.
                       At school, I was taught
a song about Jesus being the way,
the truth and the life and we made W and
T and L shapes with our hands and arms.
I remember singing it with enthusiasm
that I believed was fuelled by sarcasm, but
enthusiasm nonetheless.
The truth and the life! for apparently
we can go around claiming these things.
                       You can't always predict
what sounds will carry. Sometimes a voice
is right by my ear, clear as day, saying
Go! or Come back! or Shut! Up!
                       Heroes take turns
rescuing each other, showing up
in various iterations of the same stories. Help:
I'm trying to steal some golden fleece/
I'm trapped at the top of a burning building/
I'm falling, for my wings have melted/
I looked back and now she's gone.
            Every so often a little light floats up
            out of the dark forest like a sprite.
Give it up, Prometheus. Come and have
a snuggle on the sofa, maybe watch a movie.

How, All Right

I want to get morbid I want to get morbid
To my right there's a large window
but through it there's nothing large, nothing large
on the other side – everything's pathetic everything's pathetic
it's all so pathetically distant and out of reach . . .
Whisper in my ear something I care about or hate
Whisper wetly (I mean don't) till the hairs stand up
the hairs stand up until my eyes roll back
my fist tightens I roll back stand up
and it's all I can handle, no, I want to get morbid!
How do people smile as they go along
how is their muscle memory so toned so attuned
and ready? How can something change the world when
billions of people in complexity live without knowing it?
Have you been able to sense the tension? Everything to me
is a gleaning, i.e. painfully slow to compute, and
the ghosts in my irises flash their raincoats open
opportunely, all the possibilities I fucked up smile and wave
and dissipate, nudely. I'm so empty now! Now, knowing
all those nonliteral babies I killed! Now, soaring above to see
all those untrod paths that are crumbling over the crumbling edges
of landscapes, smashing on the rocks below! Now,
spreading womanly over this company-supplied office chair!
Now, knowing the more one learns, the worse one feels!
And yet, now, I also know nothing! I was better off before!
And before and before! I absolutely never feel sated!

Silver Lining

That low anxiety is coming back
sheepish like a silly old friend
who doesn't make life easier
but at least makes it fuller somehow.

Come in, friend, put your feet up
but not on the table where we eat.
We're looking for the silver lining
though our pillows are lumpy

and one of the animals smeared
poo on the sofa.
While we're looking, there remains
the possibility of something better.

There was a spring in my step
when I woke. I guess it's just nice
to have a bit of company. We're all
doing okay. We're doing really well.

Princes and Priests

1.
The celebrities are having mental
health breakdowns and people
are lining up for tickets.

2.
Princes and priests have done
and do things they
shouldn't.

3.
Television shows
get cancelled
and uncancelled.

4.
The disinformation activists have muddied the lawn.

5.
Some professions can be heroic
and they can be cruel.

What is the alternative?

Always, always a life
without cruelty.

6.
Everybody wants to be special,
it's a pandemic
of the individual.

It's quite incredible
how many experts we have among us.

How many self-appointed
somethings.

7.
Like flies on shit.

Like flies, on shit!

Cat

This kind of stupid cat I got last year wanders around
like she lives in a different house, sees different things
to what I see, and sometimes she sits in the hallway,
swaying slightly and gazing into space I'm not sure
is even there. She's like a lot of us, staring into the sea
of culpability waiting for absolution like fools,
unfocussed, like it's a Magic Eye and we're expecting
the dolphin of pardon to materialise. *Clickclickclick.*
I make a dolphin noise to get the cat's attention,
but she refuses. Some things are beneath us.
We find an absent middle-distance and aim for it.

Awake

Daytime, and things are
under the sun
like clouds, humans, shit
Name one new thing   you can't
Daytime does something to us
wrenches us from sleep
impolitely, terrifyingly, like being
ripped from the womb!
(or our tomb!)

I wasn't built for

what

Alien

Down across the valley the fields are painted
with circles and lines like cropmarks.
Their meaning is the same to me as alien glyphs.
At the weekends, crowds of tiny people
run around the fields, animated Lego
figurines. Sometimes their hollers sweep
up the hill and make the dogs bark half-heartedly,
like chickens. Flies hurl themselves giddy
around whatever room I'm in. Cicadas fling
themselves at my window, trying to find their tree
on the other side of the house, desperate
to join the others screeching the birds away.
This-is-OUR-tree-NOW-it's-OUR-tree-NOW.
It's a trip. They were late this year, though
the summer has been a hot one.

I'm sorry for you if you think you are not living,
if deep down you believe you've been condemned
to stay for centuries as things heat up, kind of like
getting cooked alive but so slowly you'll
probably barely notice it. I'm sorry if you think
your organs have atrophied, yet still
you walk around. Think of the stories
you'll be able to tell. How summer was not always
all year long. How snow was only high, and white.
How people played, dogs barked, bugs thrummed,
and everything except you died appropriately, with
a little mourning, with a good enough replacement.

Distant Planets

Now,
we can see
distant planets
in crisp detail,
making them
seem like our
birthright.
If all of us
stood outside and
screamed on three,
would the sound carry?
Would it make
the planets
shrivel and recoil?
Would they
release
their fiery comets
to shut us up?

What Has Changed

I'm starting to get
budget-brand headaches.
I grunt when I pick things up.
I still enter
with my upstage foot,
and though
I don't intentionally want
my whole being exposed,
here we are.
Old habits, etc.
I'm either growing
more superstitious or
I'm particularly skilled
at risk assessment.
I have upped my water intake.
I'm shocked in a hopeless way
at the vastness of the world.
I'm tired of
picking and choosing
pain that sits nicely
like a kid on the mat
who's bleeding internally,
like a blinkered horse
who is so pleased with the trophy
their scars take on a gleam –
but these days
when I try to count backwards
to send myself to sleep
I make it all the way to zero.

Crisis :(

The crisis is that our
corporeal shells are flaking. Sharp
pieces of ourselves
are scattered behind us
as we walk, so take care!

The crisis is
an inability to count the rings
that age us. When we're cut down
we're killed. R.I.P. us.
The counting's flawed anyway.

The crisis is
how we carry the metaphor
of painting over imperfections
with us into
the deepest parts of our lives.

The crisis says,
"Here's Johnny!"
every single day.
Oh, it's Johnny again.
We should have known.

The crisis reassures us when
we find out someone we thought
we should admire is, in fact,
Insufferable. One less thing
to worry about, crisis.

The crisis exposes our family jewels
as fakes. Our tears fall
on the fraudulent old glass
and turn to diamond,
slip through our fingers.

The crisis is: what do you get
if you have a roof but no walls?
Walls but no roof? Lights, but
no one's home?
No, really, what do you get?

It's a game of Would You Rather
(to which we answer,
Neither,
and sign off,
Best Wishes).

When I Think of Parties I Think of Disease

When I think of parties I think of disease.
This is what these times have done to me.

Every distance I stand to converse is a distance
too close for comfort, or it's too far to hear –

but raise a glass. Strike up the band.
Take your places on each side of the room

not according to outdated gender binaries
but whether you are exhilarated or distraught

at the thought of the freedom your life will have
when your parents are dead. Then choose your partners.

Resurrect the steps of primary school folk dances
you learnt in the hall among ghosts and sweaty hands.

Laugh in a spurt and blush at your missteps, let it
disgustingly cross your mind that wouldn't it be sweet

if your dance partner were your future spouse,
though you don't see it. No thanks, actually.

Don't do what I tell you to do. I'm a tangled ball
of old yarn, good for nothing. I wouldn't listen to me.

The way I connect any two points with my own personal
ley lines. The way I retroactively fit out

the logic of a space or memory. It's the same way
I justify myself as being either right or terrible.

By the way, that's not cream that's risen to the surface,
it's an oil slick.

Complaint

Haven't all of us ruined something?

Isn't everything terrible?

Isn't hope fleeting and utterly futile,
like trying to take
a photograph of the moon
with a cheap phone?

There was potential but you missed it.
There was connection but you blinked.
There was a lesson
but you spent it carving a dick into the desk.

The Bear

Then, after everything, the fiery bear towers in the night, their breath
fogging like phosphorescence, and
I swear I hear sizzling as their feet touch ground,
thumping closer, until we both lock our eyes on the jar of honey
sitting like an offering between us and
I want to say, *It's yours*, but my voice is stuck and
I don't speak bear, and then the bear slows
as they near the jar, one huge paw wipes foamy spittle
from their mouth, reaches down, and they growl soft
like a purr as they drink the honey like water.

//

I am visited by my sisters, who begin to talk all at once
that they worry about me here in the cave,
that I need proper heating, proper sanitation. Their eyes
well with tears so I don't tell them about the bear.
I smile at my sisters to show that I am happy. I smile
bigger and bigger and bigger until my cheeks freeze.

//

That night I wake, fevered, to find the bear
sleeping next to me. I go outside the cave to piss and
I'm worried the noise will wake them. When I return,
the bear is too still and I think they are dead.
I place a hand on their side and they sigh slow and long.
Shaking, I lie back down and catch my breath,
heart calming. I remain awake until morning.
My hand feels hot like it's touching sun-warmed fur
and my hair keeps getting in my eyes.
I'm losing the ability to tell night from day.

//

A few weeks on I make a quick wish upon waking
that the bear will live to grow old or if they're
already old then they will become older, and my
wish rushes back into me, asking
if my motives are unselfish and I cannot answer.

//

I hear terrible screaming
so I follow the sound, in case I can save somebody.
Over the hardened earth, over fallen branches, into the shade,
alongside a black stream – my skin goosebumps; I feel
not afraid but without air – into a paddock
and I find a goat whose keyhole eyes
are so blank I start to cry ferociously, like I was
always about to cry and hadn't realised. The goat
screams again, tears at the grass with its teeth and chews,
coldly, like it's not tasting anything.

//

The daffodils are out,
pursing their lips at me.
I wander back to the cave
avoiding their eyes. The bear
is sleeping, and I stand
and watch them.
They've grown smaller.
Their skin hangs looser.

//

I tried to climb a tree today, but couldn't find my footing.
My hands and legs are scraped and I'm disappointed.
If only I'd tried harder or was stronger. The bear hasn't
woken for I don't know how many days and their
breathing has slowed more than I thought possible.
I can't sleep. I'm going to wash myself
in the stream later. Once I'm clean, I'm going to lie
against the bear, for warmth. It's about time. I'm cold.

///

Highly Flammable

Autumn

When autumn hits here,
the leaves tend not to fall.

They cling and quiver in the wind
like our disappointment in them

and the few that fall go slippery and annoy us.
The light, though, thaws our cold hearts

and we don't even care we're being cheesy
for a moment or so. Who needs

a new cliché? Not us, not
when there are bigger things to worry about –

and not when it's still possible to put them aside
to look at the low shadows, the glow

of evening sun across the branches
of trees that refuse to be anything but green.

The Sky Is Bigger

If we drive slightly past our place, the hills become
bare of houses, filled with trees in every shade of dark green
like stepping back in time. The sky is bigger.
The distance hazier. The birds more rare,
and enormous and full of pluck. We have different ideas
about what makes good driving music, so we usually turn it
right down and talk instead. We both hate driving. Me because
I do it and you because you can't. We tag-team bad moods, which
is my latest, most appreciative definition of romance.
Every day I point at something and ask how long
has that been there and you always say forever.

Choose Again

Things appear
closer in the mirror.

Time folds in on itself

like those paper fortune-tellers
I made at school.

Pick a number,
lift the flap,
learn my fortune.
Choose again.

It's only paper, meaningless,
highly flammable.

//

Every few years I complete online personality tests.
They tell me I'm rare. They tell me I'm difficult
to love, or that I find it difficult to love.
They tell me I'm good at details, hate crowds.
They tell me what I've told them.

//

Shame ensures you feel
never alone, never quite at ease.
It's always close by
and at first
that was cumbersome,
but you've learnt to bear it,

like an ulcer on the inside
of your cheek
that you nibble on sometimes,
and other times stroke
with your tongue
just to know it's there.

Am I saying
there's something
comforting in shame?

I don't mean to.
Just that
you get so used to it,
it's impossible to imagine
life without it.
Would losing it create a void?

Or would it be
like stretching
and cracking your spine –
a split-second of intense relief,
only to immediately feel
the same as ever?

Do you sometimes take
a more angry bite, increasing the size
of the wound in your cheek
as punishment to yourself,
to your shame for existing,
for the reason the shame exists?

Yes, yes, yes.

//

I leave little clues. I wonder
if anyone's picking up on them,

my little breadcrumbs. I am a bird
sticking my beak between

the bars of my cage to see if the air
is purer on the outside

but nothing changes. It's all the same air.

Always Have

Once during childhood
I followed the instructions
to make a pomander.
I painstakingly stabbed
the skin of an orange
with the short stems of cloves,
gathered scented preserving powders.
I have forgotten the details.

The emotion, though – the intoxication
I felt before performing something
of an embalming – remains inside me, worries at me
as I look languidly again and again for that thrill.
You know the first piercing of orange skin,
how the tiny droplets rise in a burst,
which you can see if you're standing just right
in the sun? It smells so fresh. You might hate it.

I had to dry the pomander
in the hot-water cupboard
for so long I lost interest.
Simply wanted that tiny new thrill.
Something like gratification,
something like consolation,
like validation.
Always have.

The Illness

The illness wants itself killed/
rejoices in living, is hyperbolic;
crawls with sick bones, feathers.
Illness,
cut tunnels through muscle and limb;
itch, ache, and itch, you demon, you
glutton for punishment, masochistic
jester. Tragic, adroit fool.

//

Younger, we'd gather around the band rotunda,
National Candles pushed through card
to catch drips of hot clear wax, sing carols,
talk about eels in the lake, spot ducklings
on the water, wait for Father Christmas
to make his appearance as the wax cooled white
                    until one year
they moved it to the Bowl instead of the Park
and we perched on the grassy slopes to sing.
                We'd dream forevermore about
sliding down them, never finding our footing.

//

Anything to stop the sense of falling.

//

Anything can break the fall.

Motherchild

We see the bones through the skin.
In some lights, they're like baby birds,
so delicate it scares us. In other lights,
they're machines. Built to take over the world.

We see the skin that thickens, thins,
thickens, thins all the way till the end.
We see the bones that train the muscles,
then relent, redundant. So many

bones to be broken, so much skin to be torn,
delicate hearts to be ruined
by an accumulation of errors.
I was the child for most of my life.

I never felt able to give that up, to stop
writhing, in constant search
of the manual for living.
I'm not sure when I was at my most resilient

but it isn't now, now you can't
show me anything because it all
sucks my organs to the outside of me,
freezes skin, ruins heart.

Avoid the Swans

The wisdom was to avoid
the swans at the lake.
They could be aggressive.
If I spotted one, I'd feel a rush
of survival instinct, though
they were so elegant they
could pass as endangered.
I could have been the real threat.
They were so large and
classically beautiful I was in awe.
Almost mythological,
sleek with ulterior motives,
if what I was told was true.
An eye out for bread or
ankles to bite. I was
poised, frozen, between
information and captivation.

Mess

I like things to be a little messy.
Teeth to be a little crooked.
Cakes a little sunken.
Bench a little cluttered.
Flowers a little torn.
Clothes a little rumpled.
Acting a little stiff.
Breath a little stale.
Behaviour a little deviant.
Grass a little patchy.
Tyres a little flat.
Heroes a little fallen.
Dogs a little rabid.
Manner a little off.
Goals a little own.

Disgusting

Every now and then I get a rippling rush of vertigo

like waves of seasickness   or a flashback to
lying down too fast on a waterbed   or

an inner-ear issue

Sorry to talk about this but lately
I've been dreaming about intense messy delicious
relationships with romantic hopeless addicts and I am left

with so much longing   I want it

      like I'm in love with a past version of me

carrying around something heavy and literal in my body

It's the humidity   it's making my dreams
grimy and it turns out I'm attracted
to sour sweat   to things I shouldn't be

So much longing
for the disgusting   I yearn   I wonder what went wrong
and when   to give me this psychology
but I guess

we've all got our kinks   When does what we do
change who we are

We should die before we turn bad
before the soap writers run out of storylines
and it turns out   we were the serial killer all along
I kneel to the mess in my bedroom

I kneel to the mess in my past   to the dust   to death
which is incomprehensible   to dangerous longing   not even kidding

I kneel to the internet of vacuous memes   give it praise

I kneel to do up my laces   The dog chases the cat who

chases the fly   it's all a big misunderstanding

        each of their motives aligns to a different reality
and it nearly   breaks my heart

Walk

I go for a walk
feel the concrete through
the soles of my shoes

I carefully put
every part of myself
neatly within my body

Every Summer

As a child
summer was one continuous experience
slightly interrupted by life
Sun-warm strawberries in my palm
like baby mice
about to take their first breaths
Lying on the grass
chin to dirt
and the micro
becoming everything –
the ants at industry
the blades of grass
their city
Waves knocking the wind out of me
The salt on my skin
The nights so hot
I'd weep

Twenty years later
drinking the cheapest sparkling
acerbic wine
in the backyard in Arch Hill
Strawberry seeds
getting stuck in my crowded teeth
Feeling, again,
that the boundary fences
made my little life private
like a conversation across the room
in a sitcom
The nights so hot

I'd want to weep
but instead stayed up
until something
pulled me under

And now
at the end
of the season
I discover everything
just as I had left it
knocking the wind out of me

Mesmeriser

You want me to
           hover

You want to make me hover
as a performance of your power
              but

if my body

my own body overfilled with secrets

if my body can   be suspended
          above
if my body can
      suspend above

it's not you with the power
it's it

//

The one rule   you say
is that I have to play it up

smile then do
          pantomime-shock

as the saw   saws me

I know they expect to

see me cross-sectioned
by the metal serrations

see   pantomime-gore

(instead it's the ends
of boxes)

I expect it too

                    predict shock
will hit
            will numb my body

to the metal serrations

Maybe all this time
I've been walking around

in shock and
                    sawed

I definitely feel
like something
isn't right

//

Now for your last act
watch me   disappear

Very Many Decisions

To make a decision is to boldly decline all other options! / Every person you pass on your walks is someone to either / smile at or ignore or trip up. Every glass of water holds massive / capacity of choice: drink it, tip it into the sink, throw it on the floor, / pour it into the potplant, leave it sitting until a glittering layer of / dust settles. To read a book is to not read one million other books. / To not wet yourself is to choose privacy, to hang the washing out / is to choose piety. To focus on one star in the almost-infinite sky / is to violently reject all others, is to deny all other lifeforms, past or / present, is to submit to the limits of your eyeballs and underutilised / synapses, is to accept a smaller, more manageable day-to-day.

Viola

Viola wants to know what you want.
She says what do you want.
She pulls her hair back hard
into a ponytail, grabs it yanks it tight.
What are you looking at. Angry pimples
on her chin, sleep in her eyes, which
don't blink. She looks harder,
implying *what*. Grunts and shoves
the bottle into her baby's mouth.
Smooths the baby's hair, straightens
the baby's socks. Fuck you, she says, pushing
the pram away fast, eyes for Christmas.

Formless, Sleepless

Then, I existed as an ethereal being –
an almost-touch, a gentle-hiss exhale –
nebulous and formless, yes? Surely
there is an unease in your bones and
something about this rings true.
Surely some nights you must lie sleepless,
your mind unable to pin itself down. It's the
residue of me, a vestige defying all science,
the homeopathic dregs – have faith that I was
once enough to unsettle, at least.

Tough

Considering the absolute beauty of magnolias,
how they bloom out of branches
that appear to be dead,

fighting against metaphor while trying
to observe the natural world
in the way poets do . . . but

feeling like the cockroach
of the world, bad at dying, good at inuring
my grimy armour, scuttling around

being repellent but kind of admirable, really, almost cute.

Imaginary Den

The dogs dig urgent imaginary holes
in the furniture, essential before they curl

and curl up and settle down
to sleep, a final eye checking things out

without lifting their chins.
It's a genetic memory

of making the leaves in the den cosy.
It's like watching someone

claim they've been cured
after swallowing the placebo, but

who am I to judge. The dogs want to be
near me, seek safety and comfort in numbers,

which is no new concept but one that
gets eroded as the world devises ways

to wring value out of its inhabitants
(and inhabitants wring value out of their world).

Let me dig my little hole. Let me
settle down into it, feigning safety, let me.

Acknowledgements

Thank you to the editors of the following publications, where earlier versions of some of these poems appeared: *The Spinoff, NZ Poetry Shelf, Turbine | Kapohau, Poetry New Zealand Yearbook 2023, Stasis, Sweet Mammalian*. Gratitude to Rachel Buchanan by way of Richard Shaw's *The Forgotten Coast* (Massey University Press) for the 'past/history' concept on page 14.